John A. Cass

Is There a Hell

John A. Cass

Is There a Hell

ISBN/EAN: 9783337389970

Printed in Europe, USA, Canada, Australia, Japan

Cover: Foto ©Lupo / pixelio.de

More available books at **www.hansebooks.com**

IS THERE A HELL?

AN INQUIRY AND AN ANSWER.

BY

REV. JOHN A. CASS, A. M.

IS THERE A HELL?

I.

PRELIMINARY.

IF you will open your atlas at the map of
Africa, you will observe, at the westward of the
Nile River and Tanganyika Lake, an extensive
tract of country marked "Unexplored." The
map shows no mountains, no rivers, no lakes,
simply because no one knows what is there. It is
"unexplored." But Stanley is on his way back
to America. If, on his arrival, he should an-
nounce that, in the centre of that hitherto un-
known territory, he had discovered a great lake,
to which, on account of its dismal surroundings,
he had given some name of fearful omen, — if
such an announcement should be made by him,
two things would certainly follow.

3

1. All map-makers would henceforth indicate a lake in that region.

2. It would become known to every schoolboy by the name which Stanley gave it.

There is another land, to us all " unexplored," — the geography of which has never been written by mortals, — the land of the Hereafter. But, eighteen hundred years ago, there came to earth One who knew every rood of that territory, and who declared that *somewhere* within its boundaries is a Lake of such awful characteristics that He named it " Hell," and bade us go not near it. Now the common-sense of mankind insists upon two things here.

1. In all our maps of that country, we must somehow indicate that Lake.

2. It must be known by the name which Christ gave it — the Lake of Hell.

We may not be able to give its precise location, but the failure to give the exact latitude and longitude of a place does not prove its non-existence. Jesus Christ, and He alone, is able to inform us whether there be such a Lake; and if he affirms it, that must *some-time* end all controversy as to its existence. By general consent the Theological World is to-day asking this question : What does the Bible teach us about Hell ? It is a question freighted with the eternal interests of all souls. With solemnized minds, and hearts uplifted for divine illumination, let us seek for an answer.

Webster's Unabridged Dictionary gives the following definitions of the word " Hell."

1. " The place of the dead, or of souls after death ; the lower regions, or the grave ; called in Hebrew *Sheol*, and by the Greeks *Hades*."

2. " The place or state of punishment for the wicked after death ; the abode of evil spirits."

Commonly we employ the word in this secondary sense, but both meanings are allowable, and frequent in English. Are the Hebrew and Greek words, for which " hell " stands as equivalent, employed in the same way in the Scriptures ? "Search, and look." There are three words rendered into English by the word " hell," which we purpose to examine very carefully.

These are (1) *Sheol* — pure Hebrew — found only in the Old Testament ; (2) *Hades* — pure Greek — found in the New Testament ; (3) *Gee-Hinnom* — a compound word — found in this form in the Old Testament, and occurring in the New Testament, in the proper Grecized form, *Gehenna.**

In examining these words, if anywhere, we shall get light; for this problem as to the existence of hell is first and last a question of philology — a study of the meaning of words.

---

* We omit all discussion of the word *Tartarosas*, rendered in 2 Pet. ii. 4, " cast down to hell," as it occurs nowhere else, and when taken in connection with the context presents no difficulties. The meaning of the term " Tartarus " will be explained in the discussion of *Hades*.

II.

SHEOL.

THIS word occurs sixty-four times in the Old Testament. Thirty times it is translated by the English word " grave ; " three times by the word " pit," meaning the same as the grave ;. and thirty-one times by the word " hell."

An example of the first rendering is seen in Gen. xxxvii. 35, where Jacob said, concerning the supposed death of Joseph, " I will go down into *the grave* unto my son mourning." An example of the second is found in Num. xvi. 32, where it is said of Korah and his company, " They, and all that appertained to them, went down alive into *the pit*, and the earth closed over them, and they perished from among the congregation." An instance of the third rendering is seen in Ps. xvi. 10, where David represents Christ as saying, " Thou wilt not leave my soul in *hell ;* neither wilt thou suffer thine Holy One to see corruption ; " i. e., say all commentators, thou wilt not leave me in the *grave*, nor suffer thy consecrated Messiah to consume, or to be turned to corruption there. In other words, thou wilt raise me from the dead, before the grave exercises the power of corruption over me. So Peter construes the passage in Acts, and applies it to the resurrection of Christ from the grave.

Observe, in the first example " the grave " represents *Sheol;* in the second example " the pit " stands for *Sheol;* in the third example " hell " is put for *Sheol.* Of course " the grave," " the pit," and " hell," mean one and the same thing here. And this is true of all the sixty-four instances in which *Sheol* occurs. It never means " hell " in the sense in which we commonly use that word ; i. e., to designate a place of future misery. Professor Moses Stuart, of Andover, speaking of the word *Sheol,* says it means commonly (in fifty-nine cases out of sixty-four) " the under-world, the region of the dead, the grave, the sepulchre, the region of ghosts or departed spirits." And though Mr. S. thinks there are five passages * in which the word may hint at something *beyond the grave,*

---

* Job xxi. 13. Ps. ix. 17. Prov. v. 5; ix. 18; xxiii. 14. The reader will bear in mind that it requires some ingenuity to discover the probability above alluded to in these passages.

still he says that to assert this as more than "probable," would be "somewhat hazardous." *

Against the supposition that the Old Testament writers ever meant by using the word *Sheol* to designate a place of future retribution, stands this incontrovertible fact; viz., they had no clear knowledge of rewards or punishments in a future life. Their motives to obedience were all drawn from this world. The rewards and punishments of the Mosaic law were all temporal. Obedience was to be followed by prosperity; disobedience by adversity. The blessings for obedience to law were long life, fruitful fields, success in battle, the possession of a land flowing with milk and honey. The curses for disobedience were premature death, weakness and terror in the presence of their enemies, blighting, mildew and famine. Undoubtedly they believed in a future life, but their notions respecting it were of the vaguest sort. They conceived of *Sheol* as a place deep,† and dark,‡ having within it depths on depths,§ and fastened with gates ‖ and bars.¶ It was all-devouring,** insatia-

---

* Future Punishment.   † Job xi. 8.   ‡ Job xi. 21, 22.
§ Prov. ix. 18.   ‖ Isa. xxxviii. 10.
¶ Job xvii. 16.   ** Prov. i. 12; xxx. 16.

ble,* and remorseless,† — precisely such thoughts
as we commonly associate with the grave, — but
it had no reference to the happiness or misery of
the dead.‡

Against the supposition that the *translators* of
the Old Testament meant by using the word
" hell " to indicate a place of future retribution,
stands this fact; viz., the word " hell " did not
then § have the exclusive meaning which we commonly attach to it. The proof of this is seen in
the so-called Apostles' Creed, where it is said that
Christ, after his crucifixion, " descended into *hell*." .
Of course it does not mean that our Lord went to

---

* Isa. v. 14.

† Cant. viii. 6.

‡ We are far from saying the Hebrews had no *hopes* or *fears*
of the future. Such passages as Ps. xi. 5, 6; Isa. iii. 11,
xxxiii. 14; Ps. xxvi. 9; Isa. lxvi. 24; Ps. lxxiii. 24–26, and
others, indicate that they had vague notions concerning it, but
no clear views; especially they had no clear conception of a
place of retribution. So Jahn, Milman, and most scholars.

If *Sheol* were to be taken to represent any but a general
idea of the future, we should agree with Poole, that it " far
more often signifieth *the place of the blessed*, whither the saints
and patriarchs went when they died, than the place whither
sinners went."

§ A. D. 1611.

a place of torment, but rather that he entered the realm of death.* Webster says the word "hell" is derived from the Anglo-Saxon *helan*, to cover or conceal. To cover a thing was at first called "helling" it. Even now in Cornwall this ancient meaning is retained, and the *slating* of a house is there termed "*helling*." In Lancashire the covers of books are still called the "*helling*." This notion of covering or concealment, then, was the more common one expressed by the word "hell" in the time of James I., and when put by our translators to represent the Hebrew *Sheol* it did represent it accurately, and meant simply the grave, or the realm of the dead, as covered, hid, concealed from mortal eyes. But two centuries are sufficient for any word to acquire a different meaning from what it had at first; and so it came to pass that we, importing our modern sense of the word into the Old Testament, think we read of "hell" as a place of torment, when it only means the place or region of the dead.

* We are aware that some have tried to make out that Christ did really descend to hell, the place of torment. But the absurd idea is based upon an utterly absurd interpretation of 1 Pet. iii. 19, 20, or on an exploded and generally abandoned theory of the Atonement.

We conclude, then, that the Orthodox doctrine concerning a place of future retribution for the wicked does not rest upon the word *Sheol*, nor upon the word " hell," employed by the translators to represent it.　It is more than probable that by *Sheol* the Hebrews understood simply the realm of the dead, without any reference to their happiness or misery ; and it is eminently probable that the translators meant by using the word " hell " to represent the same idea.　Had the doctrine of future retribution no firmer support than the word *Sheol*, we should discard it instantly and forever.

III.

HADES.

THIS Greek word, translated "hell" in the New Testament, next claims our attention. It is universally allowed among critics and theologians that this word is the exact equivalent of the Hebrew *Sheol*, of which we have just treated. Of course, then, it does not mean "hell" in the sense of a place of retribution. It occurs in the New Testament only eleven times. It is ten times translated "hell," and is once rendered "grave," — in the expression, "O grave, where is thy victory?"

Before examining the passages where it occurs, let us see if we can find what the common usage of the word was in the time of our Lord's sojourn on earth. Fortunately we have all the light needed at this point.

The term *Hades* was borrowed from the old Grecian mythology, and was the name of one of its gods. It was there taught that the three sons of Saturn were Hades, Jupiter, and Neptune. Saturn had formerly ruled over all things; but in the division of the kingdom among his sons, Jupiter was made ruler of the air, and Neptune ruler of the sea, while to Hades was given dominion over the under-world, the grave, the place of the dead, the realm of departed spirits.*

Naturally the name of the mythical god *Hades* came in time to represent also the place over which he was supposed to rule, and when the myth died out from men's minds, the name *Hades* remained to indicate the abode of the dead.

But this realm of death had its divisions, or compartments, into one or other of which, according to their fitness, all souls went. The part assigned to the wicked was called Tartarus; † that of the righteous was named Elysium; while *Hades* was the general term for the realm including both Elysium and Tartarus. When the Jews came to use the Greek language, as they had done before, and continued to do after, the birth of our Saviour, they naturally employed, to express their ideas of the spirit-world, the terms which the Greeks had used to express their ideas of the same place. Hence *Hades* meant to the Jews in Christ's time

---

* So we personify Death, and speak of him as the *King* of terrors.   † 2 Pet. ii. 4.

just what it meant to the Greeks (and just what
Sheol meant to the Hebrews in Old Testament
times) — the world of the dead, the abode of departed souls. And as the Greeks divided *Hades*
into two parts, so did the Jews.* Professor
Townsend, in substance quoting Josephus, says:
" The ancient Greeks and the Jews divided *Hades*
into two parts, one division being the temporary
abode of the righteous, the other that of the wicked; the first, or upper part, was a place of happiness, though not necessarily of judicial rewards;
the other a place of suffering, though not of
judicial punishment." †

This is all in the intermediate state prior to the
resurrection and the judgment.‡ After the judgment, that part of *Hades* known as Paradise,§
where Christ promised to meet the penitent thief,
and where Abraham and Lazarus are consciously
existing, will be merged in what is known as the
New Jerusalem, — or Heaven proper, — which
shall descend from God, and into which the right-

---

* It is remarkable how little the gospel introduced new sym-
bols. The eucharist, the church, baptism, &c., are all based
upon some well-known usage, but lifted into a higher meaning.
So it is with the use of words, as we shall see further on.

† "Lost Forever."   ‡ Josephus.   § So called after the exile.

eous will be welcomed ; * while that part of *Hades*
where the wicked are now confined, will be merged
into the ultimate place of judicial punishment, —
into Gehenna, or hell proper, — amid the closing
scenes of the judgment.†

We are now prepared to look at some of the
passages in which *Hades* is found rendered into
English by the word " hell."

In Matt. xvi. 18 we read, " Upon this rock I
will build my church ; and the gates of hell shall
not prevail against it." *Hades* is the word rendered " hell," and the obvious meaning is that the
church shall never see death, shall never cease to
exist.   In Matt. xi. 23, Christ declares that Caper-
naum, which, on account of his residence there, had
been exalted to heaven in point of privilege, should
also be brought down to " hell," where evidently the
word means destruction ; for certainly the city had
not been lifted to heaven, nor did it ever after
come down to hell, in the sense in which we use
those terms.   Rev. vi. 8 has these words : " And
I looked, and behold, a pale horse : and his name

---

* Rev. xxi. 1–7.   Matt. xxv. 34.

† Rev. xx. 13, 14.   Matt. xxv. 41.   Townsend, slightly
changed.

that sat on him was Death, and Hell followed with him." " Hell " here is simply *Hades*, the realm of the dead, and the imagery employed is that of a terrible warrior going forth to kill, and send men to the spirit-world. And so of all the eleven instances in which the word *Hades* occurs, it invariably means the region of the dead, or the abode of departed spirits, without any reference to their happiness or misery. It is precisely equivalent to *Sheol* among the Hebrews, and never means " hell " in the sense of a place of final retribution.

The Orthodox doctrine concerning future retribution does not rest upon this word *Hades*, nor upon the term " hell " which represents it in English.* If it had no firmer base than this, we should discard the doctrine at once and forever, and cry anathemas upon the men who teach it.

---

* We are not unmindful of Luke xvi. 23. *Hades* is the term here used, and Dives is said to be in torment. But obviously he was not yet in Gehenna fire. He was not utterly abandoned, as the request concerning his brethren indicates. He was simply enduring the normal consequences of a life of sin. Lazarus is represented in that part of *Hades* called Paradise, while the general term is used to designate the place of the rich man. Dives was not in hell, the place of final retribution. (Townsend, in " Lost Forever.")

2

IV.

GEHENNA.

So far we have found no hell of misery for lost souls. Shall we find any? Two of the words which are sometimes translated " hell " have been shown to mean the region of the dead, the abode of departed spirits. Cannot the remaining word be shown to have the same meaning? Would God it might be so. Heaven and earth should join in one eternal hallelujah if it could be shown that the remaining word *Gehenna* had no other meaning. O, what unutterable joy would come to a thousand homes, from which some unsaved ones have gone into eternity, if it could be shown that there is no eternal misery in *Gehenna!* But this cannot be shown. The fair scheme of so-called Universal Salvation is shivered to atoms on this rock. All the wisdom of the ages has failed, so far, to escape the obvious meaning of this awful word. No argument has ever fallen from lip or pen which can for one moment satisfy an unprejudiced inquirer after truth. We find no doctrine of hell in *Sheol ;* we find no future misery taught by the word *Hades ;* but *Gehenna* does teach the doctrine of a hell of endless misery. GEHENNA! Upon this word the doctrine rests immovably firm. GEHENNA! From this awful word shoot forth the lurid flames of perdition. GEHENNA! In its echoes we hear the wails of lost souls. GEHENNA! In the presence of this word of fearful omen let us lay aside all dogmatic assertion, and reverently seek to learn the truth.

What does the word mean? All men are agreed that *Gehenna* is the Greek form of the Hebrew words *Gee-Hinnom,* and that it literally means "the valley of Hinnom." This was a pleasant valley at the south of Jerusalem by the brook Kedron. Here, in ancient times and under idolatrous kings, the worship of Moloch, the idol-god of the Ammonites, was practised. The head of this idol was like that of an ox, while the rest of its body resembled that of a man. The image was hollow, and was heated by fire before the sacrifice began. Then young children were laid in its arms and actually roasted alive — offered thus in sacrifice to Moloch. The place was sometimes called Tophet,* from a word meaning Tympanum, because in those sacrifices the priests beat violently the tympana, lest the shrieks of the dying children should disturb the worshippers. But when these horrible rites were abolished by Josiah, and the Jews began again to worship God, they detested this valley as the scene of their awful guilt. Josiah caused to be carried there all the filth and offal of Jerusalem, and the place was desecrated, and made one of loathing and horror. For above six hundred years it had been regarded by the Jews as the common lay-stall of Jerusalem — a receptacle into which they threw every species of filth, as well as the carcasses of animals, and the dead bodies of executed criminals. To prevent the pollution of the air from this mass of decaying matter, fires were kept incessantly burning from the beginning to the end of the year. Hence came the phrase " The fires of Gehenna." And as the offal would breed worms, as all putrefying meat does, there also arose the expression " Where the worm dieth not."

To the Jewish mind this valley was associated

* In Jeremiah.

with all that was most fearful, horrible, and appalling; and was the fittest symbol on earth to
represent the place of future retribution, in the
existence of which they now fully believed.*　It
is now agreed by most men, — theologians, critics, historians, and poets, whether Christian or
infidel, — and is beyond successful contradiction
from any man, that during our Lord's sojourn
on earth, and for at least two hundred years
prior to his advent, the Jews employed the phrase
" valley of Hinnom " as a symbol of the fearful
retribution of the future world ; and when, in
conformity to their law,† they cast an apostate‡
Israelite into its filth and flame, all men knew
that in like manner God would cast his soul into
a *Gehenna* of misery in another world.　And now
let it be noted and pondered : This valley, with

* When this idea took definite shape in their minds is not
known.　Probably at some period between the close of the Old
Testament canon and the year 200 B. C.　Stuart thinks it may
have been handed down by tradition from some period even
earlier.　See also Universalist writers : Fernald, Hanscom,
Whittemore, and Balfour.

† Matt. v. 22.

‡ Apostasy in a Theocracy is high-treason — a crime punishable with death in all well-ordered governments.

all its sickening and horrible associations, was
seized upon by Jesus Christ, and by him made
to represent the place and condition of all wicked
men in the world to come, precisely as the Jews
did then employ, and for hundreds of years had
employed it in all their speech concerning the
hereafter. Ay, let it be noted and pondered yet
again : He who left his bright home in Glory to
die for man ; He whose advent in human form
was heralded by angelic music and blazing star ;
He who spent his life in healing the sick, in
comforting the sorrowing, and in doing good ; He
who told us of the home of many mansions ; He
who left his pathway from the manger to Geth-
semane marked with tears, and from Gethsem-
ane to Calvary with blood ; He whose tender,
compassionate soul cried out, while on the Cross,
for his murderers, " Father, forgive them, for they
know not what they do," — yea, even He, our
Saviour, Brother, Friend, and Teacher of all
teachers, " who came to correct all false notions,
seized upon this term, and, without qualification,
used it in all its appalling significance to designate the place of future and endless retribution."

Turn we then to note the cases where the

Master used the word — the fearful word — *Gehenna*.

It occurs in the New Testament twelve times, and in every instance is rendered into English by the word "hell." That it means, in each case, a place of future misery, is clear to any unprejudiced mind.

The Sermon on the Mount furnishes three examples of its use. Matt. v. 21, 22, reads: "Ye have heard that it was said by them of old time, Thou shalt not kill; and whosoever shall kill shall be in danger of the judgment: But I say unto you, That whosoever is angry with his brother without a cause shall be in danger of the judgment: and whosoever shall say to his brother, Raca, shall be in danger of the council: but whosoever shall say, Thou fool, shall be in danger of hell-fire." Clarke says: "There are three offences here which exceed each other in their degrees of guilt. 1. *Anger* against a man accompanied with some injurious act." For this a man was liable to be brought before the "judgment," or Jewish court of twenty-three, which could inflict the punishment of strangling.

"2. *Contempt*, expressed by the opprobrious epithet *raca*, or shallow-brains." For this one could be summoned before the "Council," or Sanhedrin, to receive sentence of death by stoning.

"*Hatred* and *mortal* enmity expressed by the term *moreh*, or apostate, where such apostasy could not be proven." For this offence one could be burnt alive in the valley of Hinnom.*

These facts were well known by the people to whom our Lord was speaking. But is he simply telling them what they already knew about Jewish law? Would such utterances have caused the people to be "astonished" at his teaching? Surely not. Every man who heard him, knew that Christ was speaking of purely *spiritual* matters. What is meant, then, must be that God will punish men in a future world with different degrees of severity, such as were symbolized by the several modes of punishment employed among the Jews. Stuart well says of this: "It seems impossible to give the passage any other rational, defensible meaning. It follows, of course, that though Gehenna is here referred to in its lit-

---

* It will be remembered that apostasy, high-treason, was punishable with death. Here it is seen that if the charge was not proven, the penalty was inflicted upon the accuser.

eral sense, yet the meaning of the whole passage does not permit us to understand the idea intended to be conveyed as a literal one. It is employed as a source of imagery, to describe the punishment of a future world, which the Judge of all hearts and intentions will inflict."

Again, in verses 29, 30, of this same chapter, Christ says that, if one's right hand or right eye should offend, or cause him to sin, it were better to cut off the hand, or pluck out the eye, and so avoid sinning, than to retain both and be cast into "hell." *Gehenna* is the word. But "most certainly this cannot be understood of a *literal casting into Gehenna;* for who was to execute such a punishment? Not the Jewish courts, for they had no knowledge of the offence which a man's right hand or right eye moved him to commit; i. e., they could not call in question and punish a member of the human body because it tempted its owner to sin. It must then be a punishment which God would inflict. But was this ·a literal casting in the " valley of Hinnom "? *

* Stuart.

In Matt. xxiii. 15 we find Christ saying that the Scribes and Pharisees would compass sea and land to make one proselyte, and that when he had been gained, he would be "twofold more a child of Gehenna" than his proselyters; i. e., he would, because more wicked than they, be doubly deserving the punishment of hell. Surely no one will take this as a literal reference to the valley of Hinnom,-for there never existed a practice, or a law authorizing the practice, of casting a man into that valley of fire because he had by change of views become a Pharisee.

In Matt. xxiii. 30, Christ says: "How can ye (Scribes and Pharisees) escape the damnation of Gehenna?" Does he mean to ask, "How can ye escape being cast alive into the valley of Hinnom?" Were they in any danger of such punishment? Nay; but they were the most powerful and most popular party in Jerusalem. But when we remember that they were so intensely wicked that Jesus called them "whited sepulchres," and "a generation of vipers," it becomes clear that they were in danger of suffering the torments of hell in another world.

Passing the other examples, which are equally

clear with those now quoted, we select for the
last passage Matt. x. 28 : " Fear not them which
kill the body, but are not able to kill the soul:
but rather fear him which is able to destroy both
soul and body in hell." *Gehenna* is the word.
" Destroy both soul and body in *Gehenna!*"
The body might indeed be burned in that awful
valley; but could the soul — the immaterial and
immortal soul — be destroyed there? It must
be obvious to the most cursory reader, and to
the profoundest searcher of this text, that Christ
here speaks of *Gehenna* in another world, into
which God is able to cast the soul. The " hell"
of this verse is so evidently real, though future,
that no man can reason it out of existence.

Now, then, what have we learned in our study
thus far?

1. That *Sheol*, in the Old Testament sometimes
translated " hell," does not mean a place of future
misery, but simply the region of the dead, the
abode of departed spirits, without any reference
to their happiness or misery; and that the doctrine of a place of future retribution does not
rest on this word.

2. That *Hades*, in the New Testament some-

times translated " hell," does not mean a place of future misery, but simply the region of the dead, the abode of departed spirits, without any reference to their happiness or misery; and that the doctrine of a place of future retribution does not rest on this word.

3. That *Gehenna*, in the New Testament uniformly translated " hell," does mean, in every instance, a place of future misery; and that the doctrine of a place of future retribution does rest on this word as a chief corner-stone.

Gehenna becomes, then, the most blood-curdling word in human speech, and is but faintly represented by our word " hell" with all its horrible associations.

V.

FURTHERMORE.

ON one point let us not be misunderstood. We are not engaged in controversy — in trying to establish the fact of a hell against any who deny it — but we are simply declaring the revelation of God. Few men to-day entertain any doubt about it, and most are agreed that we must indicate such a lake on our maps of the future world.

Who are agreed concerning it?

1. The Evangelical Church, under whatever name, on all the globe.

2. The Roman Catholic Church, in all lands.

. 3. The Greek Church, holding sway over countless acres of earth, and millions of men.

4. All prominent Infidels and Skeptics in all lands and in all time. Such men as Paine in America, Hume in England, and Renan in France, have declared that the Bible does teach the existence of hell.

5. The Universalist Church. Mr. Balfour, in his "Inquiry," says: "Most Universalists have

conceded this to their opponents, that there is a place of future punishment. Winchester, Murray, Chauncey, Huntington, and others, all admit that there is a place of future punishment, and that the name of it is Hell." *

6. It is the commonly received opinion in the Unitarian Church.

7. It is involved, of necessity, in the creeds of all, of whatever name, who hold to the doctrine of Restorationism, or the graduation into happiness after a period of suffering in the future world.

Who deny that there is a hell?

1. A very few among the Second Adventists — the more ignorant of them.

2. A handful of gross Materialists of no religious belief.

3. A few lisping Sentimentalists, whose only *argument* is, " O, what a horrible thought! It cannot be possible there is a hell."

None others. All men who read the Bible with their eyes open do see in it the doctrine of a future

---

* And after correspondence with some of the leading men of that church at the present time, and personal conversation with others, we fail to find any who are bold enough to deny its existence, — though they say but little about it.

hell. Whether it be eternal in duration, is a matter which we reserve for future discussion. But be it eternal, or to exist only for a year, it behooves every soul to shun it, for it is the most fearful place in all God's universe. Human language is impotent to describe it, and Jehovah himself represents it by the *figure* of a lake burning with fire and brimstone, in which are Satan, the fallen angels, and the false prophets; the fearful, the unbelieving, and the abominable, with thieves, and drunkards, and murderers, and whoremongers, and sorcerers, and idolaters, and all liars; and the condition of its inhabitants is so appalling that it is called in Scripture " the second death."

Reader, is it not a fair inference from all this, that no mortal man, no archangel from Glory, no arch-fiend from Perdition, can picture it too darkly, or with too much emphasis or plainness of speech, warn us to fly to Christ for salvation, that we may escape being cast into Hell?

IS THERE A HELL?

INQUIRY AND AN ANSWER.

BY

REV. JOHN A. CASS, A. M.